C000199524

HERITAGE TRACTION ON THE MAIN LINE

HERITAGE TRACTION ON THE MAIN LINE

Fred Kerr

PEN & SWORD
TRANSPORT

First published in Great Britain in 2018 by
Pen & Sword Transport
An imprint of
Pen & Sword Books Ltd
47 Church Street
Barnsley
South Yorkshire
S70 2AS

Copyright © Fred Kerr 2018

ISBN 978 1 52671 312 4

The right of Fred Kerr to be identified as Author of this work has
been asserted by him in accordance with the Copyright, Designs and Patents
Act 1988.

A CIP catalogue record for this book is
available from the British Library.

All rights reserved. No part of this book may be reproduced or transmitted
in any form or by any means, electronic or mechanical including photocopying,
recording or by any information storage and retrieval system, without
permission from the Publisher in writing.

Typeset in 11pt Minion by Mac Style Ltd, Bridlington, East Yorkshire
Printed and bound in India by Replika Press Pvt Ltd

Pen & Sword Books Limited incorporates the imprints of Atlas, Archaeology, Aviation, Discovery, Family History,
Fiction, History, Maritime, Military, Military Classics, Politics, Select, Transport, True Crime, Air World,
Frontline Publishing, Leo Cooper, Remember When, Seaforth Publishing, The Praetorian Press,
Wharncliffe Local History, Wharncliffe Transport, Wharncliffe True Crime and White Owl.

For a complete list of Pen & Sword titles please contact
PEN & SWORD BOOKS LIMITED
47 Church Street, Barnsley, South Yorkshire, S70 2AS, England
E-mail: enquiries@pen-and-sword.co.uk
Website: www.pen-and-sword.co.uk

Front Cover: Class 37/4 37403 *Isle of Mull* has been restored by the Scottish Railways Preservation Society (SRPS) Diesel Group at its Bo'ness base but was hired by DRS in 2016 for an initial period of six months to complement its Class 37/4 fleet. On 5 August 2016 the locomotive stormed through Brock whilst working the 10:05 Preston–Barrow service as part of the Cumbrian Coast diagrams.

Rear Cover: GBRf Class 73/2 73201 *Broadlands* awaits departure from Southport on 29 March 2014 with a Network Rail Inspection train to Ormskirk via Sandhills, working in top 'n tail mode with Network Rail Class 73/1 73138.

Contents

Locomotive Owners and Operators..8

Class 20 – English Electric Company..10

Class 31 – Brush Traction..14

Class 33 – Birmingham RC&W..20

Class 37 – English Electric Company..24

Class 40 – English Electric Company..32

Class 43 – BR Workshops..34

Classes 44 thru 46 – BR Workshops..38

Class 47 – Brush Traction..39

Class 50 – English Electric Company..65

Class 52 – BR Workshops..72

Class 55 – English Electric Company..78

Class 56 – Brush Traction; BR Workshops..88

Class 57 – Brush Traction..96

Class 60 – Brush Traction..108

Class 73 – BR Eastleigh C&W; English Electric Company..110

Class 86 – BR Doncaster; English Electric Company..114

Class 87 – BREL Crewe..120

Class 89 – Brush Traction/BR Workshops..123

Class 92 – Brush Traction..124

British Railways was privatised in 1994 under the Railways Act 1993, which included the right of any locomotive owner/operator to operate locomotive(s) on the national network subject to them being fitted with the necessary equipment to work trains and being approved by Network Rail to be fit to do so. Whilst this right was geared to the continued operation of steam traction, it also opened the door to the owners of modern traction (both diesel and electric) to operate their locomotives subject to meeting the same operating conditions.

In the early days of Privatisation the rolling stock, including locomotives, was vested in Rolling Stock Companies (ROSCOs) who then leased stock to the individual Train Operating Companies (TOCs). This did not apply to the Freight Companies which had been organised into two companies (Railfreight Distribution (RfD) and Trainload Freight (TLF)) as a prelude to Privatisation; their consequent sales to new owners included the locomotives hence these never became part of the ROSCO assets.

The onset of Privatisation encouraged new railway companies which serviced niche markets such as Train Operation (TO) with Direct Rail Services (DRS) and its commitment to nuclear flask movements being one of the successful TOs. These new operators sought to reduce start-up costs by either hiring preserved locomotives, as exemplified by Cardiff Valley Railways (CVR) hiring locomotives for peak-hour services, or by buying withdrawn/stored locomotives, as exemplified by DRS.

The purchase of locomotives for either preservation (including potential main-line use) or re-use by other operators makes it difficult to qualify the status of individual locomotives, hence the term 'heritage traction' has been frequently used instead to identify locomotives by age rather than ownership/usage. In this album that age delineation has been set at twenty years, but note that the term 'heritage traction' also defines such locomotives sold (or hired) after Privatisation to a second owner/operator in addition to those already preserved.

During the early part of the twenty-first century 'heritage traction' was the mainstay of niche operators such as DRS and West Coast Railway Company (WCRC) whilst existing operators such as GB Railfreight (GBRf) proved willing to use 'heritage traction' when the need arose. Later new operators such as Colas Railfreight also found it economic to use 'heritage traction' to establish their business before committing to the purchase of more modern locomotives to service an established business.

This album has not considered the fortunes of diesel shunting locomotives, as their operations are committed more to industrial usage rather than the main line, but seeks to illustrate the variety of main line locomotives which were able to continue working on the national network within the framework of the Railways Act 1993. This album also notes the rise and fall of some of the new companies through changes of locomotive ownership; a case in point being Class 47/8 47832, which has been operated by four companies (Fragonset; Victa Rail; DRS; WCRC) since being withdrawn from service by First Great Western in 2004.

Fred Kerr, October 2017

Class 20/0 D8056 was hired by Earles Cement from Harry Needle Railway Company (HNRC) to transfer wagons between the cement works and the interchange siding at Earles Sidings; on 22 July 2003 D8056 shunts a loaded train from the works site into the siding.

Locomotive Owners and Operators

Preserved Locomotive Owners

The Railways Act 1993 created a legislative framework that allowed the use of privately-owned locomotives subject to them meeting specific operating standards set by the Office of Rail Regulation (ORR) and being approved to operate by Network Rail (as successor to Railtrack). Whilst the rules were geared to the continued use of steam traction, they also provided the opportunity to use preserved diesel/electric locomotives on the national network subject to them also meeting the same regulations.

Companies Using Heritage Traction

Privatisation sought to encourage new companies to enter the railway industry and, of those which entered the area of train operations, some started up by hiring/buying locomotives from existing companies. Locomotive ownership may differ from the locomotive operator, even where the locomotive carries the operator's livery; where possible ownership of the locomotive will be identified within the appropriate caption(s). Some of the new operators encouraged by Privatisation are identified in this album and include:

Advenza Freight – a freight company that became part of Cotswold Rail in 2005

Colas Railfreight – a French company that began operating in the UK in 2007 and initially hired locomotives before buying Class 47/56 locomotives to build up its business

Cotswold Rail – initially a rolling stock seller that bought Class 47s then provided 'Thunderbird' services to East Anglian TOCs. It bought Advenza Freight in 2005 but tax problems with the latter company in 2009 forced both companies into administration in 2010

Devon & Cornwall Railways (DCR) – began operation in 2008 as part of the British and America Railway Services (BARS) set up by the USA-based Iowa Pacific Holdings company; as at December 2016 DCR provides 'spot hire' traction for rolling stock moves

Direct Rail services (DRS) – set up in 1996, initially as a provider of transport services to the nuclear industry, but has expanded into commercial freight and passenger services

Electric Traction Services (ETS) – a commercial company set up by the **AC Locomotive Group (ACLG)** (a registered charity) to undertake 'spot hire' of electric locomotives; it was subsequently 'absorbed' by Europhoenix in 2015

Europhoenix – a commercial company set up by the **AC Locomotive Group (ACLG)** (a registered charity) to restore and sell diesel and electric locomotives abroad; after 'absorbing' ETS it began operating as a 'spot hirer' of locomotives – initially to ROGS

FastLine – was set up by Jarvis, a railway contractor, when it expanded into train operations in 2006 but ceased operations when Jarvis entered administration in 2010

Fragonset – began operations in 1997 as a 'spot hire' company with 4 Class 47 locomotives but by 2002 it operated 75 locomotives, some owned by private individuals. In 2005 it merged with Merlin to form FM Rail but the new company entered administration in December 2006; it was subsequently resuscitated as Nemesis Rail in 2007

GB Railfreight (GBRf) – was founded as a freight company in 1999 but has expanded its services over time to include a passenger licence. Although it owns new locomotives the company is known for using preserved locomotives on a 'spot hire' basis as and when the need arises

Harry Needle Railway Company (HNRC) – was founded in 1998 for 'spot hire' and locomotive repair/maintenance – mainly of shunting locomotives. This has expanded into main line locomotives and continues to be one of the company's activities as at December 2016

Nemesis Rail – was established in 2007 to undertake mainly coaching stock maintenance but retains some of the locomotives rescued from the demise of FM Rail (see Fragonset) to provide 'spot hire' facilities

Network Rail – was set up to replace Railtrack in October 2002 to maintain the infrastructure; it normally hires locomotives to work its inspection trains but owns a number of locomotives for specific purposes

Rail Operations Group Services (ROGS) – was set up in 2015 to provide locomotives for stock movements; at present it both hires heritage traction (from Europhoenix) and is buying heritage traction (Classes 37 and 47) as it builds up its business

UK Rail Leasings (UKRL) – was formed in 2013 by owners of Class 56 locomotives to provide 'spot hire' locomotives

West Coast Railway Company (WCRC) – was formed in 1998 to provide both charter hire and locomotive 'spot hire' based on its fleet of Classes 37 and 47 locomotives.

Locomotives are stabled at Tonbridge West and a visit to the location on 8 June 2005 noted locomotives operated by three companies; Class 33/2 33202 *Meteor* bears Fragonset livery; Class 73/2 73206 *Lisa*; 73204 *Janice* and 73209 *Alison* bear GBRf livery and, at the rear, Class 73/2 73212 and 73213 bear the livery of Railtrack. The Railtrack operations had been dissolved in 2002 and this pair of locomotives were being operated by Network Rail as successor to Railtrack.

Class 20 – English Electric Company

Builder
English Electric (Vulcan Foundry); English Electric (Robert Stephenson Hawthorn (RSH) Darlington)

Year Built
1957–68

Engine
English Electric 8SVT rated at 1000 hp @ 850 rpm

Transmission
Electric

BR Fleet Numbers
D8000–8199; 8300–8327; TOPS = 20001–20228

TOPS Classification: The introduction of TOPS in the late 1960s and its application to Fleet Operations from 1974 allowed various sub-groups to be identified:

20/0 = Standard fleet
20/3 = 20301–20305 dedicated to Railfreight duty at Peak Forest but the project was cancelled and the locomotives regained their standard fleet numbers
20/3 = 20301–20315 refurbished locomotives bought by Direct Rail Services (DRS) in 1995–1996
20/9 = 20901–20906 refurbished locomotives bought by Hunslet-Barclay for weed-killing services in 1989 and subsequently bought by DRS and – later – HNRC

Class 20/0 20142 + 20189 are owned by Michael Owen who operates as 20189 Ltd as at 2016 to offer the locomotives for 'spot hire' workings. Left: This included working a North Wales charity railtour on 27 July 2013 organised by GBRf when 20189 (in London Transport red livery) piloted 20142 (in BR Corporate blue livery) on the Llandudno–Llandudno Junction leg of a Llandudno–Holyhead supplementary charter as they passed Deganwy whilst, right, 20142 piloted 20189 past Balshaw Lane Junction on 14 April 2016 whilst moving barrier coaches from Wolverton Works to Craigentinny as part of a stock move on behalf of ROGS.

The DRS Class 20/3 fleet was dedicated to the transport services of the nuclear industry.

20312 + 20315 pass Leyland on 10 June 2003 with a Sellafield–Crewe consist that includes the transfer of Class 37/6 37612 + 37607 to Crewe Gresty Bridge depot.

20310 + 20313 trundle past Brock on 13 June 2008 whilst working a Crewe–Sellafield service.

20305 works in top 'n tail mode with 20301 *Max Joule 1958–1998* on 2 September 2003 as they pass Arnside with the weekly Runcorn–Sellafield chemical train.

In their latter years the Class 20/3s were used on the seasonal Rail Head Treatment Trains (RHTT), based at York where their light axle-load proved valuable for the local branch lines. On 26 October 2012 20301 *Max Joule 1958–1998* passes Copmanthorpe with the Grimsby–Malton leg of the daily circuit, working in top 'n tail mode with 20303.

In 2012 DRS began withdrawing its Class 20/3 fleet but 20311 + 20314 were obtained by HNRC to add to the Class 20 hire fleet that was being established to meet a GBRf contract for the movement of London Transport stock.

The HNRC duo were hired by GBRf to power a staff excursion on 27 July 2013 from Cardiff to Llandudno and were noted approaching Llandudno working in top 'n tail mode with Class 20/0 20142 + 20189.

On 24 April 2013 the duo formed the rear of the Old Dalby–Amersham stock move as they passed Portway with Class 20/9 20901 + 20905 (in GBRf livery) leading the consist.

Prior to the GBRf contract the duo were contracted to transfer stock from Kilmarnock to Laira, here noted passing Brock on 22 August 2012.

20311 had passed Buckshaw on 21 August 2012, working to Kilmarnock in top 'n tail mode with 20314, having collected barrier wagons from Washwood Heath.

The GBRf contract for stock movements involves transfers between Bombardier's Derby Works to Old Dalby (for testing); from Old Dalby to Amersham (thence West Ruislip for delivery) and from West Ruislip to Derby for rectification/modifications. HNRC has supplied 8 Class 20 locomotives (20096/107/118/132/311/314/901/905); each transfer involves two pairs of locomotives working in top 'n tail mode and each pair carries a different livery. On 24 April 2013 the Old Dalby–Amersham stock move passed Portway powered by Class 20/9 20901 + 20905 (in GBRF livery) working in top 'n tail mode with Class 20/3 20311 + 20314 (in HNRC Orange livery).

Class 31 – Brush Traction

Builder
Brush Traction

Year Built
1957–1962

Engine
English Electric 12SVT rated at 1470 hp @ 850 rpm

Transmission
Electric

BR Fleet Numbers
D5500–5519 (TOPS = 31001–019); D5520–5699; D5800–5862; TOPS = 31101–31327; 31400–31470; 31500–31570 (with gaps)

TOPS Classification: The introduction of TOPS in the late 1960s and its application to Fleet Operations from 1974 allowed various sub-groups to be identified:

30.0 = D5500–5519 with original Mirrlees engine (no TOPS number ever carried)
30.1 = D5520–5699; 5800–5862 with original Mirrlees engine (no TOPS number ever carried)
31.0 = D5500–5519 (TOPS = 31001–31019)
31.1 = D5520–5699; 5800–5862 (TOPS = 31101–31327)
31.4 = 31400–31470 Random locomotives fitted with Electric Train Heating equipment (ETH)
31.5 = Class 31.4 locomotives transferred to Civil Engineers Department with ETH equipment removed/disconnected
31.6 = 31601–31602 Class 31.1 locomotives fitted with through ETH cables

DCR Class 31/6 31601 pilots DCR Class 31/4 31454 as they pass Settle on 2 March 2011 whilst working a Lincoln–Carlisle charter.

Left: Class 31/6 31601 *Bletchley Park Station X* approaches Fairwood Junction, under the shadow of the Wiltshire White Horse, on 9 June 2004 whilst working a Bristol–Weymouth service in top 'n tail mode with 31452 *Minotaur*. Both locos were on hire to Wessex Trains (WT) from Fragonset but only 31601 received the WT pink livery.

Below Left: DCR Class 31/6 31601 *Devon Diesel Society* carries the latest DCR grey livery on 14 July 2015 as it passes Winwick en route from Bo'ness to Crewe CS for its next stock move working.

Below Right: DCR Class 31/6 31601 *Gauge O Guild 1956–2006* passes Portway on 26 June 2008 hauling a Network Rail (NR) consist of Class 31/1 31105 and 31233 from Gloucester to the NR base at Derby; despite Wessex Trains being no longer in business, the locomotive still carries that company's livery.

Class 31/6 31602 has operated with more than one train company including:

Below: Bearing the name of *Chimera* when hired by Fragonset to First Group to work a Chester–Blackpool North circuit in top 'n tail mode with Class 31/4 31459 *Cerberus* – noted passing Chew Moor on 29 March 2004.

Bottom: Bearing the name of *Driver Dave Green* when hired by DCR to Network Rail and noted passing Balshaw Lane Junction on 5 September 2011 with a Derby RTC–Carlisle working.

Right: Bearing the name *Chimera* when hired by FM Rail to First Group to work a Chester–Blackpool North circuit in top 'n tail mode with Class 31/4 31459 *Cerberus* – noted curving through Chorley on 20 May 2005.

During its brief existence Fragonset had a number of Class 31 locomotives available for hire, including:

Right: Class 31/1 31106 *Spalding Town* seen arriving at Bamber Bridge on 4 May 2002 pilotting Class 33/1 33108 whilst working a Carnforth–Peterborough charter. Of interest is that 31106 was owned by railway journalist Howard Johnson but hired to/operated by Fragonset.

Below Left: Class 31/4 31454 working in top 'n tail mode with Class 31/1 31128 *Charybdis* on 8 June 2004 as they approach Fairwood Junction with a Bristol–Weymouth service. Both locomotives were on hire from Fragonset to Wessex Trains to supplement the DMU fleet on summer dated services.

Below Right: Class 31/1 31128 *Charybdis* noted at Preston in the company of Class 31/4 31454 *The Heart of Wessex* on 20 January 2007 awaiting the return to Birmingham of a Merrymaker charter. At this point in time FM Rail, the locomotives' 'owner' had just entered administration and the future fate of both locomotives was uncertain.

A regular operator of Class 31 locomotives is Network Rail which continues to use them on various inspection services up to December 2016; they are easily identified by their Corporate Yellow livery. Examples of them at work, passing through the Warrington–Preston area include:

Class 31/1 31105 propelling a Crewe–Morecambe service through Winwick on 6 March 2008.

Class 31/1 31233 propelling a consist led by Driving Brake Second Open (DBSO) vehicle 9701 onto the West Coast Main Line at Winwick on 10 July 2014 whilst working a Derby–Carlisle service.

Class 31/4 31465 passing Balshaw Lane Junction on 8 January 2014 whilst propelling a Derby RTC–Carnforth service led by DBSO 9701.

Class 31/1 31233 curving through Winwick on 27 April 2016 whilst transferring a faulty coach from Carlisle to Derby RTC for repairs.

Following the collapse of FM Rail, the locomotive fleet still continued to be hired for stock movements as on 30 August 2007 when Class 31/4 31459 *Cerberus* was hired from Nemesis Rail to move a pair of Class 507 trainsets from Birkenhead North–Crewe IED for wheel turning following the failure of MerseyRail's wheel lathe.

Class 33 – Birmingham RC&W

Builder
Birmingham RC&W

Year Built
1960–1962

Engine
Sulzer 8LDA28A rated at 1550 hp @ 750 rpm

Transmission
Electric

BR Fleet Numbers
D6500–6597; TOPS = 33001–33065; 33101–33119; 33201–33212

TOPS Classification: The introduction of TOPS in the late 1960s and its application to Fleet Operations from 1974 allowed various sub-groups to be identified:

33.0 = D6500–6585 (TOPS = 33001–33065) Standard locomotive
33.1 = Random locomotives fitted with push-pull equipment (TOPS = 33101–33119)
33.2 = D6586–6597 (TOPS = 33201–33212) Hastings gauge

Right: Fragonset Class 33/1 33108 is pilotted by Fragonset Class 31/1 31106 *Spalding Town* on 4 May 2002 as they call at Bamber Bridge with a Carnforth–Peterborough charter.

Below: FM Rail Class 33/1 33103 *Swordfish* stables in Clapham Junction carriage sidings on 2 September 2005 awaiting its next duty.

In 2001 DRS bought four withdrawn Class 33 locomotives (33025/029/030/207) for a project which failed to materialise but, in the short time that they operated for the company, they were frequently used to power the weekly chemical train that operated between Sellafield and Runcorn's chemical complex.

Below: Class 33/0 33030 + 33025 stand on the Runcorn Branch on 20 August 2002 awaiting permission to enter the Folly Lane site where their journey ends.

Class 33/0 33025 is the rear of the Runcorn–Sellafield service on 6 May 2003 as it passes Catterall working in top 'n tail mode with Class 33/0 33030. Note that 33025 carries Intermodal branding for a project that failed to succeed beyond a trial period.

Class 33/0 33030 leads Class 33/2 33207 as they pass Leyland on 10 June 2003 with the Runcorn–Sellafield service.

Class 33/2 33207 works in top 'n tail mode with Class 33/0 33025 as they cross the River Kent at Arnside on 15 July 2003 whilst working the Runcorn–Sellafield service.

Following the cancellation of the project, DRS elected to exchange its (Sulzer-engined) Class 33 fleet for (English Electric-engined) Class 37s owned by WCRC; the latter company soon found work for Class 33/2 33207 which was quickly re-liveried in WCRC's Maroon livery.

Left: Class 33/2 33207 carries WCRC Maroon livery on 3 April 2006 as it passes Leyland whilst working in multiple with Class 33/0 33029 powering a Derby–Carnforth (WCRC) stock move. Note that 33029 still carries DRS livery.

Below: To mark the end of locomotive haulage on the Rhymney–Cardiff Peak Hours services, Arriva Trains Wales organised a 'Farewell to Rhymney Locomotive Haulage' day with a special timetable using examples of locomotive classes that had seen service throughout the previous decade. WCRC provided Class 33/2 33207 and Class 47/8 47854, seen here approaching Gilfach on 4 December 2005 whilst working in top 'n tail mode with a Rhymney–Cardiff service.

Class 37 – English Electric Company

Builder
English Electric (Vulcan Foundry); English Electric (Robert Stephenson Hawthorn (RSH) Darlington)

Year Built
1960–1965

Engine
English Electric 12CSVT rated at 1750 hp @ 850 rpm

Transmission
Electric

BR Fleet Numbers
D6600–6608; D6700–6999; TOPS = 37001–37308
See also TOPS notes below

TOPS Classification: The introduction of TOPS in the late 1960s and its application to Fleet Operations from 1974 allowed various sub-groups to be identified:

37.0 = D6600–6608; D6700–6999; TOPS = 37001–37308

Sub-groups created for specific purposes in the 1980s include:

37.3 = 37310–37314 + 37320–37326 for Hunterston steel traffic
37330–37335 + 37340–37345 with CP7 bogies for Sandite duties
37350–37359 + 37370–37384 with CP7 bogies for Departmental duties
37.4 = 37401–37431 with ETH for secondary passenger duties
37.5 = 37501–37521 for Steel Sector duties
37667–37699 for Railfreight duties
37.6 = 37601–37612 for Eurostar duties (later cancelled and subsequently bought by DRS)
37.7 = 37701–37899 (with gaps) for Coal and Steel Sector duties
37.9 = 37901–37904 with Mirrlees MB275T rated at 1800 hp @ 1000 rpm; 37905–37906 with Ruston RK270T rated at 1800 hp @ 900 rpm; both sub-groups were allocated to the Steel Sector based at Cardiff to compare engine performance
97.3 = 97301–97304 for Network Rail to test ETRMS for Cambrian Line services

An early buyer of Class 37 locomotives was DRS which bought large numbers of both Class 20 and 37 locomotives to start up the business, noting that the commonalty of engine parts would help minimise costs whilst providing a reliable locomotive fleet – given the experience of BR and the successor operators in the Privatisation era.

Class 37/6 37608 pilots Class 20/3 20314 on 22 April 2003 as they approach Arnside with a Sellafield–Crewe working.

DRS Class 37/0 37218 powers through Brock on 16 June 2015 whilst working a Preston–Barrow service in top 'n tail mode with DRS Class 37/4 37402 *Stephen Middlemore 23.12.1954–8.6.2013.*

DRS Class 37/5 37667 arrives in Southport on 18 September 2012 with the Manchester Victoria–Southport leg of a Civil Engineers inspection service being worked in top 'n tail mode with DRS Class 37/0 37194 at the rear.

DRS Class 37/0 37259 + DRS Class 57/0 57004 curve through Oubeck on 7 May 2014 whilst working a Crewe–Sellafield flask service.

DRS Class 37/5 37682 passes Winwick on 15 January 2013 with a Derby RTC–Carlisle Network Rail service being worked in top 'n tail mode with Network Rail Class 31/4 31465.

In 2015 DRS successfully concluded negotiations to provide additional train services along the Furness Coast between Carlisle and Barrow, with the first southbound weekday service extended to Preston and for which it sought Class 37/4 locomotives to provide the necessary traction.

Left: 37401 *Mary Queen of Scots* carries BR's large logo livery as it enters Arnside on 8 August 2015 whilst working a Saturday Carlisle–Barrow–Lancaster service in top 'n tail mode with Class 37/4 37402 *Stephen Middlemore 23.12.1954–8.6.2013.*

Below Left: To supplement the Class 37/4 fleet, DRS hired Class 37/4 37403 *Isle of Mull* from the Scottish Railway Preservation Society (SRPS) Diesel Group and it is seen passing Brock on 5 August 2016 heading north with a Preston–Barrow service.

Below Right: Earlier, DRS had sought to build up the charter side of its business and this led to it buying withdrawn Class 37/4 locomotives for such passenger duties. On 20 June 2008 37423 climbed through Euxton with the Carnforth (WCRC)–Derby ecs (empty coaching stock) move that would form a charter train the following day.

The changing fortunes of new operators led to a change of ownership of some locomotives, as noted with the operation of Class 31 locomotives. A similar situation arose with Class 37 locomotives, given their reputation as a true mixed traffic locomotive; an example of this is Class 37/0 37261 whose different ownerships are illustrated.

37261 was finally stored in January 2014 and moved to HNRC's Barrow Hill site for component recovery a month later. This was suspended and in July 2015 the locomotive entered preservation with the SRPS at Bo'ness where it is intended to restore the locomotive to working order for possible main line service.

Right: Initially bought by Ian Riley Engineering (IRE), it was restored to service as support for his main line steam locomotive fleet specially to haul the locomotives between locations and heritage lines. It was sold to WCRC in May 2004 and on 2 November 2004 still bore the BR Green livery applied by IRE when it was hired with WCRC Class 37/0 37197 to move fire-damaged Class 175 'Coradia' trainset 175008 *Valhalla Blackpool Pleasure Beach* from Preston station to the Ribble Steam Railway (RSR) where the damaged vehicle could be loaded onto a lorry for onward transit to the repairers. 37261 is seen at the rear of the ensemble as the consist entered the RSR's 'estate'.

Below Left: Following its sale to WCRC in May 2004 it was repainted into WCRC livery in early 2005 and joined the pool of locomotives dedicated to the burgeoning ROYAL SCOTSMAN luxury service. On 19 June 2005 it was paired with FM Rail Class 31/1 31190 *Gryphon* as they passed Arrivan with the Bridge of Orchy–Taynuilt ecs stage of the weekend tour.

Below Right: 37261 was subsequently transferred to DRS as part of a locomotive exchange and, in November 2007, was one of the pool locomotives powering the North Wales Rail Head Treatment Trains (RHTT) service. On 15 November 2007 37261 worked the Crewe–Holyhead service in top 'n tail mode with DRS Class 37/0 37194 as the consist passed Dwygyfylchi.

The DRS fleet included the complete pool of 12 Class 37/6 locomotives which found use on both flask and charter services.

37604 forms the rear of the Preston–Ormskirk leg of *THE LANCS LINK* charter on 7 March 2015 as DRS Class 37/4 37419 *Carl Haviland 1954–2012* leads the consist when it passes Meadow Lane.

37610 *TS (Ted) Cassady 14.5.61–6.4.08* pilots DRS Class 37/0 37059 through Winwick on 22 April 2016 whilst working an Eastleigh–Carlisle charter.

37610 *TS (Ted) Cassady 14.5.61–6.4.08* + DRS Class 37/0 37218 drift through Balshaw Lane Junction on 12 February 2016 with a Crewe–Sellafield service.

37609, in top 'n tail mode with 37606, is at the rear of the Sellafield–Heysham service as they enter the Heysham site on 16 November 2006 for an exchange of flasks.

WCRC uses its pool of Class 37 locomotives for stock movements and train support as on 2 May 2012 when Class 37/5 37516 was at the rear of the main line steam test being undertaken by B1 Class 4-6-0 1306 *Mayflower* as the consist approached Longpreston.

Above Left: During the 2016 'Scarborough Spa Express' season the train was powered by WCRC diesel traction between Carnforth and York where steam traction took over. On 23 June 2016 the diesel traction was supplied by Class 37/5 37668 + 37669, here passing Lostock Hall Junction on the outward journey.

Above Right: WCRC Class 37/5 37676 *Loch Rannoch* + 37685 power through Brock on 6 November 2010 as they work in top 'n tail mode with Class 47/8 47804 whilst powering a Birmingham–Edinburgh charter on behalf of Spitfire Railtours.

Left: WCRC Class 37/7 37712 curves through Clitheroe on 16 July 2008 whilst working a Carnforth–Manchester Victoria Diner Special in top 'n tail mode with WCRC Class 47/7 47787 to celebrate the retirement of a prominent local railwayman.

In addition to DRS and WCRC, the Class 37 locomotives have found favour with other operators.

An early HNRC hire locomotive was Class 37/0 37194 noted passing Leyland on 26 March 2003 whilst en route from Carnforth (WCRC) to Derby; this locomotive was subsequently sold on to DRS.

In 2008 HNRC supplied Network Rail with 4 Class 37 locomotives (re-designated Class 97/3) to trial the new ERTMS system on the Cambrian lines west of Shrewsbury; on 28 January 2009 97304 *John Tiley* passed Portway whilst on Barrow Hill–Shrewsbury route-learning duty.

During the 2013 'Jacobite' season Ian Riley bought Class 37/5 37518 to act as standby locomotive at Fort William; on 21 June 2013 the locomotive was 'fired up' in preparation to shunt the stock of the returning afternoon 'Jacobite' service. This locomotive was subsequently bought by WCRC at the end of the 2013 operating season.

In 2015 ROGS was formed to service the niche market of stock transfers and initially hired Class 37 locomotives from Europhoenix. On 12 February 2016 Class 37/7 37884, bearing Europhoenix branding, passed Balshaw Lane Junction with a stock move of HST vehicles from Kilmarnock to the Great Central Railway via the connection at East Leake.

Class 40 – English Electric Company

Builder
English Electric (Vulcan Foundry); English Electric (Robert Stephenson Hawthorn (RSH) Darlington)

Year Built
1958–1962

Engine
English Electric 16-cylinder 16SVT Mk II rated at 2000 hp @ 850 rpm

Transmission
Electric

BR Fleet Numbers
D200–399; TOPS = 40001–199

Top: Class 40 D345/40145 is owned by the Class 40 Preservation Society (CFPS), based on the East Lancashire Railway. The CFPS is one of the locomotive owners which seeks to operate a locomotive on the main line and has selected D345 from the locomotives under its stewardship to do so. After preparing the locomotive for main line working, a test run was required which took place on 28 October 2002 with the test train passing Winwick en route from Carnforth to Crewe accompanied by Ian Riley's Class 37/0 37038 as insurance in case of failure. The test proved successful thus enabling the CFPS to organise a small number of tours to raise funds for the continued support of the CFPS fleet.

Right: The locomotive, temporarily named *East Lancashire Railway*, was hired by John Fishwick, a Preston local transport operator, on 28 July 2007 to power the Manchester Victoria–Preston leg of a Manchester–Carlisle charter, run to commemorate the centenary of the company's operations, and was noted passing Buckshaw, later to become Buckshaw Parkway, on the outward journey.

The first railtour was operated from Birmingham to Holyhead on 30 November 2002 and D345 is seen curving through Abergele & Pensarn station on the outward journey.

D345 has also operated in BR Corporate blue livery as on 29 November 2014 when it powered a Southport–York charter, working in top 'n tail mode with WCRC Class 47/8 47804. D345 eases its train through the approach to St Lukes on the outward journey.

Its main-line certification is useful when visiting rail-connected centres as a Gala visitor especially when it can haul locomotives between centres – as on 26 June 2008 when D345, temporarily named *East Lancashire Railway* and bearing large logo livery with TOPS Number 40445, passed Portway hauling Class 37/9 37901 *Mirrlees Pioneer* and 37906 from Kidderminster (Severn Valley Railway) to the Midland Railway Centre to take part in a Diesel Gala a few days later.

Standing in Southport station after its return from York.

Class 43 – BR Workshops

Builder
BR Crewe

Year Built
1976–1982

Engine
MTU 16V4000R41R rated at 2250 hp @ 1500 rpm (see note below)

Transmission
Electric

BR Fleet Numbers
43002–43198

Note: These 'locomotives' are Power Cars which operate in top 'n tail mode with 8/9 coach trainsets and were originally fitted with Paxman Valenta engines. When re-engined, the post-Privatisation train operators adopted different strategies:

1. **First Great Western** began re-engining in 2005 and adopted the MTU engine but retained the Power Car fleet numbers
2. **East Coast** followed on but added 200 to the Power Car fleet numbers to identify those which had been re-engined
3. **East Midland Trains** decided to re-engine with the Paxman 12VP185 engine rated at 2100 hp @ 1500 rpm
4. **Grand Central Trains** opted for the MTU engine but since its fleet differed from the main fleet by being fitted with buffers it elected to renumber the Power Car fleet numbers to 434xx where 'xx' was the final digits of the original fleet number

When Virgin Trains replaced its Inter City/HST trainsets Porterbrook and Angel Trains offered the Power Cars for re-lease. First Great Western were able to buy some of these but Network Rail leased 3 vehicles (43013/014/062) from Porterbrook for high-speed infrastructure monitoring whilst Grand Central Trains leased 6 vehicles from Angel Trains (43065/43067/43068/43080/43084/43123) to provide its Sunderland–Kings Cross service.

Left: 43014 *The Railway Observer*/43062 *John Armitt* curve through Winwick on 27 April 2016 with the weekly Craigentinny CS–Crewe CS inspection train.

Right: 43014 *The Railway Observer*/43062 *John Armitt* power past Euxton on 17 August 2016 with the weekly Craigentinny CS–Crewe CS inspection train.

Below: 43062 *John Armitt* is the rear of the inspection train on 26 August 2016 when it passes Dawlish en route from Penzance to Bristol St Phillips Marsh depot.

Prior to re-engining
the Grand Central
Power Cars bore
unlined black livery
as noted on:

9 March 2009 when
43084 led a Sunderland–
Kings Cross service past
Colton.

19 February 2009 when
43068 led a Kings Cross–
Sunderland service past
Colton.

When re-engined (and
renumbered) the Power
Cars received an orange
stripe as noted by 43480
when it passed Colton
on 27 October 2015 as
the rear vehicle of a
Kings Cross–Sunderland
service.

The Power Cars leased to Grand Central were those fitted with buffers which had been fitted in the early days of the ECML Electrification Scheme to work with Class 822xx series Driving Van Trailers whilst the Class 91 locomotives were being built.

Right: 43468 leads a Kings Cross–Sunderland service past Copmanthorpe on 25 June 2016.

Below Left: 43484 *Peter Fox 1942–2011 Platform 5* leads a Kings Cross–Sunderland service on its approach to Colton Junction on 25 June 2016.

Below Right: 43484 *Peter Fox 1942–2011 Platform 5* leads a Sunderland–Kings Cross service past Colton on 24 September 2015.

Classes 44 thru 46 – BR Workshops

Builder
BR Crewe; BR Derby

Year Built
1960–1963

Engine
Sulzer 12LDA28B rated at 2500 hp @ 750 rpm (see note below)

Transmission
Electric

BR Fleet Numbers
D1–10 (TOPS = 44001–44010); D11–137 (TOPS = 45001–45077; 45101–45150); D138–193 (TOPS = 46001–46056)

TOPS Classification: The introduction of TOPS in the late 1960s and its application to Fleet Operations from 1974 allowed the three classes, whilst similar in external features, to be separately identified:

44.0 = D1–10 Original Pilot Scheme locomotives with Sulzer 12LDA28 engine rated at 2300 hp @ 750 rpm and disc indicators
45.0 = D11–137 with headcode boxes; D11–31 + D68–107 with split headcode and D32–67 + D108–137 with 4-character headcode

As TOPS numbering was being applied, fifty locomotives were selected in random order for fitting with Electrical Train Heat (ETH) equipment resulting in:-

45.0 = locomotives with either steam heat or no heat (following removal of boiler)
45.1 = locomotives with Electric Train Heat (ETH)
46.0 = D138–193 (TOPS = 46001–46056) locomotives with Brush electrical equipment replacing Crompton Parkinson electrical equipment

Although 2 x Class 44, 11 x Class 45 (all variants) and 3 x Class 46 have been preserved, only 45112 and 46035 have seen main-line service. 45112 was bought by a private owner involved with Fragonset which operated the locomotive. The owner continued his involvement with Fragonset and its successors (FM Rail; Nemesis Rail) and the locomotive was made available to successor companies until early 2007 when its lack of OTMR (On Train Monitoring and Recording) equipment led to its withdrawal from the main line. As at 2016, 45112 sees regular use as shed pilot at the Burton on Trent base of Nemesis Rail.

Class 45/1 45112 *The Royal Army Ordnance Corps* climbs through Leyland on 20 March 2002 with an ECS working from Carnforth (WCRC) to Hathersage.

Class 47 – Brush Traction

Builder
Brush Traction; BR Crewe

Year Built
1962–1967

Engine
Sulzer 12LDA28C rated at 2580 hp @ 750 rpm (initially 2750 hp @ 800 rpm but de-rated following engine problems)

Transmission
Electric

BR Fleet Numbers
D1100–1111; D1500–1999; TOPS = See note below

TOPS Classification: The introduction of TOPS in the late 1960s and its application to Fleet Operations from 1974 allowed various sub-groups, whilst similar in external appearance, to be separately identified:

47.0 = 47001–47299 locomotives with steam or no heat; some examples have Slow Speed Equipment for MGR duties
47.3 = 47300–47381 locomotives designed for freight duties with no heat equipment but fitted with Slow Speed Equipment for MGR duties

47.4 = D1500–1519 (47401–47420) the original locomotives fitted with ETH equipment from new
47421–47600; 47602–47665 locomotives retrospectively fitted with improved ETH equipment
47671–47677 as 47421 *et alia* but regeared for Highland Line/Sleeper duties
47.6 = 47601 – test bed locomotive for Class 56
47.7 = 47701–47716 locomotives converted for Edinburgh-Glasgow (later ScotRail) push-pull services
47721–47793 locomotives converted for Rail Express Systems (RES) duties including charter services
47798–47799 locomotives dedicated to Royal Train duties with security equipment fitted
47.8 = 47801–47854 refurbished Class 47/4 and 47/7 (RES) locomotives with increased fuel capacity for long range duties
47.9 = 47901 – test bed locomotive for Class 58
47971–47976 locomotives transferred to Departmental duties
48.0 = D1702–1706 initially fitted with Sulzer 12LVA24 engine rated at 2650 hp @ 1050 rpm but restored to Class 47/0 specification in the early 1970s prior to TOPS numbering

When withdrawn from network service many Class 47 locomotives were bought for further main line duties; one such buyer was Riviera Trains which was primarily a coaching stock supplier to the charter market but purchased Class 47 locomotives for both haulage and 'spot hire' contracts. On 6 October 2006 the Riviera Trains duo of Class 47/ 8 47843 *Vulcan* + 47805 *Talisman* was hired by DRS to power its Sellafield–Sandbach–Sellafield chemical service, here noted passing Balshaw Lane Junction on the return working.

Opposite page

When withdrawn from network service in 2002, Class 47/0 47237 was leased to DRS in April 2003 and was noted passing Winwick on 20 March 2007 with a Kingmoor–Crewe stock move.

This page

Right: In 2007 the locomotive was sold to Cotswold Rail which branded it for its Advenza Freight operation. On 26 June 2008 47237 drifted through Portway with a Gloucester–Stockton service of empty scrap wagons to service the Stockton–Cardiff Tidal contract that the company had gained.

Below Right: When Advenza Freight entered administration at the end of 2009 its locomotive fleet was put up for sale and 47237 was bought by WCRC to join its growing fleet of Class 47 traction. On 7 September 2011 47237 arrived at Southport, working in top 'n tail mode with Class 47/8 47804, bringing the empty stock of a charter service that 47804 would work forward.

Below Left: 47237 carries WCRC Maroon livery and branding on 18 August 2016 when it piloted WCRC Class 37/5 37669 on the Carnforth–York leg of the seasonal 'Scarborough Spa Express' whilst passing Lostock Hall Junction on the outward journey.

Cotswold Rail's Class 47/8 47813 *John Peel* + Class 47/7 47714 (in Anglia Trains livery whilst contracted as a 'Thunderbird' locomotive) power through Euxton on 3 June 2006 with a mixed rake of stock working a return charter from Carlisle to Stafford.

Above Left: Cotswold Rail's Class 47/3 47316 *Cam Peak* + Class 47/8 47813 curve through Winwick on 17 September 2005 whilst working a Wolverhampton–Edinburgh charter.

Above Right: Cotswold Rail's Class 47/8 47813 *John Peel* coasts through Settle on 1 December 2005 with a stock move from MOD Longton to Derby that includes four Porterbrook Class 821xx Driving Van Trailers (DVTs) being returned from Virgin Trains.

Left: Cotswold Rail's Class 47/8 47828 *Joe Strummer* + 47813 *John Peel* race through Euxton Junction on 24 March 2007 with a Watford Junction–Carlisle Pullman charter.

An early 'spot hire' operator was Fragonset Railways (FR) which began operations by buying 4 Class 47 locomotives from the liquidated charter business operated by Pete Waterman; by 2002 the FR fleet comprised 75 locomotives. In 2005 FR merged with Merlin Rail to form FM Rail but this was a brief merger that ended in liquidation at the end of 2006.

Left: Fragonset Class 47/7 47703 *Hermes* eases out of Southport on 14 April 2004 with a Railtrack inspection train returning to Manchester Piccadilly.

Below Left: FM Rail Class 47/7 47709 is the rear of a Carlisle–Oxenholme ecs move on 3 September 2005, powered by Class 47/3 47355 *Avocet*, where it will collect passengers for its return to Euston.

Below Right: FM Rail Class 47/7 47709 *Dionysus* works in top 'n tail mode with FM Rail Class 47/7 47712 *Artemis* on 15 July 2006 as they pass Deganwy with a Pullman charter returning from Llandudno to Euston. FM Rail had ceased trading at this time and this service was being operated by DRS which had bought the Pullman operation as part of its move into charter operations.

FM Rail Class 47/3 47355 *Avocet* curves through Docker on 3 September 2005 working in top 'n tail mode with Class 47/7 47709 *Dionysus* as they power an empty stock service from Carlisle to Oxenholme where the train would collect passengers for the onward return to Euston.

The Stratford Class 47 Group (SCFG) bought Class 47/7 47732 in March 2007 and restored it to an earlier condition as Class 47/4 47580 *County of Essex*. Once restored in June 2008 the group elected to return it to main line service by hiring it to WCRC, with whom it has operated a large number of services.

Left: 47580 *County of Essex* eases through Euxton on 6 August 2011, working in top 'n tail mode with WCRC Class 47/7 47760, as they power a charter returning from Ravenglass to Wolverhampton.

Below: 47580 *County of Essex* is in top 'n tail mode with WCRC Class 47/0 47270 *Swift* as they curve into Southport on 2 May 2011 whilst powering the stock of a charter that will be hauled from Southport by 47270.

Bottom: 47580 *County of Essex* climbs away from Settle on 2 June 2012 whilst working a Newport–Carlisle charter in top 'n tail mode with WCRC Class 47/8 47854 *Diamond Jubilee*.

47580 *County of Essex* speeds through Bamber Bridge on 25 May 2013 whilst working a Lincoln–Carlisle charter in top 'n tail mode with WCRC Class 47/7 47760.

47580 *County of Essex* approaches Galabank Junction as it returns from Tweedbank to Edinburgh on 15 May 2016 with A3 Class 4-6-2 60103 *Flying Scotsman* attached at the rear.

47580 *County of Essex* passes Balshaw Lane Junction on 14 April 2016 with a Southall–Carnforth (WCRC) stock move that includes 'Battle of Britain' Class 4-6-2 34067 *Tangmere* and WCRC Class 47/7 47760 *Chris Fudge 29.7.70–22.6.10*.

47580 *County of Essex* works in top 'n tail mode with WCRC Class 47/7 47760 as it approaches St Lukes on 29 May 2013 with a Southport–Holyhead charter.

WCRC Class 47/4 47500 pilots 'Britannia' Class 4-6-2 70000 *Britannia* through Acton Bridge on 9 November 2010 whilst returning to Crewe after 70000 had undergone a light engine test run to Warrington following overhaul at the Crewe Heritage Centre.

WCRC Class 47/7 47760 races through Brock on 1 July 2011 with a Carnforth (WCRC) stock move to Crewe CS for a charter the following day.

Left: WCRC Class 47/7 47760 shunts stock at Hellifield on 5 February 2009 prior to taking the trainset back to Carnforth (WCRC).

Right: WCRC Class 47/0 47245 is the rear of the FELLSMAN (Lancaster–Blackburn–Carlisle) service on 30 July 2014 as it passes Bamber Bridge behind Stanier 8F 2-8-0 48151.

WCRC Class 47/0 47245 curves through Oubeck on 10 June 2006 whilst working a Glenrothes–Chester charter in top 'n tail mode with WCRC Class 47/8 47851 *Traction Magazine*.

WCRC Class 47/8 47804 + WCRC Class 47/7 47786 *Roy Castle OBE* curve through Beckfoot on 10 September 2014 whilst working a Carnforth (WCRC)–Bo'ness stock move.

WCRC Class 47/8 47826 *Springburn* retains its BR Inter City livery on 29 December 2005, despite its recent purchase by WCRC, as it passes Selside forming the rear of a Bedford–Carlisle charter.

WCRC Class 47/8 47826 carries WCRC Maroon livery on 6 June 2011 as it forms the rear of a Carnforth (WCRC)–Crewe CS stock move. The 'advertising' on the bodyside arose from a dispute with Network Rail which refused permission for WCRC to erect a hoarding to advertise its seasonal 'Scarborough Spa' service hence WCRC applied the advert to the locomotive that was being stabled at the site where the hoarding was to have been located.

51

DRS Class 47/4 47501 *Craftsman* approaches Maryport on 10 December 2009 whilst working in top 'n tail mode with DRS Class 37/6 37610 *TS (Ted) Cassady 14-5-61 to 6-4-08* on the 12:20 Workington–Maryport 'Floodex' service.

DRS Class 47/4 47501 *Craftsman* curves through Winwick on 15 January 2013 whilst working a Carnforth (WCRC)–Stoke stock move in top 'n tail mode with DRS Class 47/8 47818 as a prelude to driver training duty between Crewe and Stoke on Trent.

Riviera Trains Class 47/8 47812 + 47847 curve through Leyland on 3 October 2006 whilst on hire to DRS to work the Runcorn–Sellafield chemical service.

Vintage Trains, based at Tyseley, bought Class 47/7 D1755/47773 to be used for support purposes in conjunction with its railtour programme, either by providing train heat or assisting with shunt moves as required.

47773 passes Balshaw Lane Junction on 1 March 2008 with a stock train that had Class 86/2 86259 Les Ross at its rear following a Preston–Crewe–Liverpool circuit to present 86259 on the front of a Birmingham–Preston charter for its return journey to Tyseley.

Following the first run of a Class 86/2 to Hadfield on 20 December 2008 (see page 118), 47773 was used to draw the consist of locomotive and stock back to Manchester Piccadilly from where the train returned to Birmingham behind Class 86/2 86259 *Les Ross*; the train is seen taking the direct line at Dinting to avoid the need to reverse at Glossop on its return journey to Manchester Piccadilly.

The dedicated duo of Class 47/7 locomotives retained for Royal Duty are used for 'normal' duties when not required.

Royal Class 47/7 47798 *Prince William* passes Winwick on 18 September 2002 with a Leeds–Hereford VSOE (Venice-Simplon Orient Express) charter.

Royal Class 47/7 47799 *Prince Henry* passes Winwick on 28 October 2002 with a Butterley–Carnforth (WCRC) 'Royal Scotsman' stock move.

The start-up of Colas Railfreight as a UK railway operator began with its hire of locomotives until it purchased 3 Class 47/7 locomotives.

This page

Right: Colas Class 47/7 47727 *Rebecca* + 47749 *Demelza* drift through Portway on 2 July 2009 with a Burton on Trent–Dollands Moor steel train; the steel was subsequently shipped through Boston leading to a regular Washwood Heath–Boston service being established.

Below Left: Colas Rail Class 47/7 47727 *Rebecca* + Porterbrook Class 57/3 57314 power through Euxton on 24 July 2009 with the daily Carlisle–Chirk timber service. 57314 carries Arriva Trains Wales livery as it had been on hire to that company for the Cardiff–Holyhead service until replaced by Class 67 locomotives.

Below Right: Colas Rail Class 47/7 47749 *Robin of Templecombe* pilots Colas Rail Class 66/8 66843 through Euxton on 10 May 2010 whilst working the daily Carlisle–Chirk timber service.

Opposite page

DRS Class 47/7 47790 *Galloway Princess* curves past Flimby on 1 December 2009 whilst working in top 'n tail mode with DRS Class 37/4 37423 *Spirit of the Lakes* on the 11:45 Maryport–Workington 'Floodex' service.

Whilst primarily a freight operator, DRS obtained a passenger licence in order to operate charter services; this licence proved useful in 2009 when the company was funded by the government to operate a free rail service ('Floodex') between Maryport and Workington following flood damage which included washing away the road bridge in Workington that connected the town to points north.

DRS Class 47/7 47712 *Pride of Carlisle* works in top 'n tail mode with DRS Class 57/0 57007 as they approach Maryport on 25 May 2010 with the 10:30 Workington–Maryport 'Floodex' service.

DRS Class 47/8 47805 works in top 'n tail mode with DRS Class 47/8 47810 *Peter Bath MBE 1927–2006* as they climb through Euxton on 5 September 2012 with the Carlisle–Manchester Victoria leg of the 'AFRICA EXPRESS' which was chartered by musicians for a rail-borne tour of Britain.

DRS Class 47/8 47802 climbs through Greenholme on 28 July 2006 en route to Carlisle whilst undertaking driver training on passenger trains between Carnforth and Carlisle.

DRS Class 47/8 47810 *Peter Bath MBE 1927–2006* works in top 'n tail mode with DRS Class 57/3 57308 *County of Staffordshire* on 6 July 2014 as they power through Eastwood with a Bradford Interchange–Blackburn shuttle service run in conjunction with the Tour de France cycle race.

An example of multi-ownership is exemplified by Class 47/8 47832 which was operated by First Great Western at Privatisation and owned by the Porterbrook Leasing Company. It was first sold to Fragonset in August 2004 and received Fragonset livery but in August 2007 was operated by Victa Westlink Rail and received that company's livery. The company only retained the locomotive for a short while before it was bought by DRS in December 2007. When DRS began to withdraw its Class 47/8 fleet on receipt of the Class 68 fleet, 47832 was sold on in 2015 to WCRC which then repainted it into the company's Maroon livery.

Right: 47832 bears the Victa Westlink Rail branding and livery as it passes Clitheroe on 25 August 2007 pilotted by Riviera Trains Class 47/8 47839 *Pegasus* whilst powering a Holyhead–Carlisle charter.

Below Left: 47832 bears DRS Compass livery on 14 April 2010 as it pilots DRS Class 47/4 47501 *Craftsman* whilst passing Siddick powering the 15:10 Maryport–Workington 'Floodex' service in top 'n tail mode with Porterbrook-owned DRS-operated Class 57/0 57012.

When DRS gained the contract to haul the VSOE 'Northern Belle' charter programme, a condition of the contract was that the locomotives should match the coaching stock by bearing Pullman livery. DRS selected Class 47/7 47790 *Galloway Princess* and Class 47/8 47832 to be the dedicated locomotives for this service.

Below Right: 47832 *Solway Princess* bears the 'Northern Belle' Pullman livery as it passes Euxton on 20 August 2012 working in top 'n tail mode with DRS Class 47/7 47790 *Galloway Princess* hauling an Edinburgh–Euston 'Northern Belle' charter.

DRS Class 47/7 47790 *Galloway Princess* bears 'Northern Belle' Pullman livery as it passes Buckshaw Parkway on 22 November 2014, working in top 'n tail mode with DRS Class 47/8 47818, whilst working a Manchester Victoria–Preston service chartered by Northern Trains to provide extra trains for Christmas shopping in Manchester.

Left: Arriva Trains Wales ceased operating locomotive haulage of Rhymney–Cardiff services in December 2005 and ran a 'Farewell to Rhymney Locomotive Haulage' timetable on 4 December 2005 when trains were hauled by locomotive types that had worked services during the previous decade. WCRC provided two locomotives for the event; WCRC Class 33/2 33207 and Class 47/8 47854, here noted leaving Pontlottyn on a Rhymney–Cardiff service operating in top 'n tail mode with 47854 leading.

Above: Riviera Trains Class 47/8 47815 *Abertawe* + 47839 pass Euxton on 4 August 2006, whilst on hire to DRS, powering a Mossend–Daventry inter-modal service.

Below: DRS Class 47818 curves through the approach to Chorley on 6 December 2014 whilst working in top 'n tail mode with DRS Class 47/8 47853 *Rail Express* as they power a Buckshaw Parkway–Manchester Victoria Christmas Shoppers extra chartered by Northern Trains.

Above: Bearing original WCRC Maroon livery with black diamond stripe, WCRC Class 47/8 47854 accelerates through Bamber Bridge on 8 May 2004 with a Preston–Carlisle charter on behalf of St James Parish Church. This annual charity charter is operated by WCRC to various destinations that originate from Carnforth.

Right: Bearing the early WCRC Maroon livery with black diamond stripe, WCRC Class 47/8 47854 passes Coed Kernow on 29 February 2004 whilst approaching Cardiff with a Bolton–Cardiff Rugby special.

Below: Bearing the later plain Maroon livery, WCRC Class 47/8 47851 joins the main line at Balshaw Lane Junction on 13 July 2016 whilst working a Harrogate–Blaenau Ffestiniog charter in top 'n tail mode with WCRC Class 57/3 57313.

Class 50 – English Electric Company

Builder
English Electric (Vulcan Foundry)

Year Built
1967–1968

Engine
English Electric 16-cylinder 16CSVT rated at 2700 hp @ 850 rpm

Transmission
Electric

BR Fleet Numbers
D400–449; TOPS = 50001–50050

Note: Nineteen locomotives from this class have been preserved with many owners hopeful of returning them to main line service. Most, however, are based on heritage lines where their main activities are regular use on timetabled services albeit at the heritage line speed limit of 25 mph rather than their designed speed of 100 mph.

Preserved Class 50 50049 *Defiance* works in top 'n tail mode with EWS Class 37/4 37411 *Caerphilly Castle/ Castell Caerphili* on 4 December 2005 as they curve into Gilfach with a Cardiff–Rhymney service during the 'Farewell to Rhymney Locomotive Haulage' celebrations.

Preserved Class 50s 50031 *Hood* + 50049 *Defiance* curve into Preston on 16 June 2006 whilst working a Swindon–Inverness charter.

Preserved Class 50 50031 *Hood* works in top 'n tail mode with EWS Class 37/4 37411 *Caerphilly Castle/Castell Caerphili* as it departs from Pontlottyn on 4 December 2005 with a Cardiff–Rhymney service during the 'Farewell to Rhymney Locomotive Haulage' celebrations.

Preserved Class 50s 50031 *Hood* + 50049 *Defiance* curve through Leyland on 16 December 2006 with a Cardiff–Leeds charter routed via the WCML; Carnforth; Hellifield and Leeds.

On 16 December 2006 preserved Class 50s 50031 *Hood* + 50049 *Defiance* worked a charter from Cardiff to Leeds via the WCML to Carnforth then via the Little North Western route to Hellifield thence Leeds. The duo are noted curving away from Hellifield en route to Leeds whilst (opposite) they were noted approaching Settle Junction earlier on the outward journey.

The duo were noted curving away from Hellifield whilst earlier they were noted approaching Settle Junction on the outward journey.

Preserved Class 50s 50049 *Defiance* + 50031 *Hood* curve through Onibury on 16 August 2003 with a charter returning from Chester to Reading via the Marches Line.

Preserved Class 50s 50049 *Defiance* + 50031 *Hood* race past Forton on 4 March 2005 whilst working a Swindon–Fort William charter.

Preserved Class 50 50049 *Defiance*, working in top 'n tail mode with EWS Class 37/4 37411 *Caerphilly Castle/Castell Caerphili*, approaches Pontlottyn with a Cardiff–Rhymney service on 4 December 2005 during the 'Farewell to Rhymney Locomotive Haulage' event.

Class 52 – BR Workshops

Builder
BR Crewe; BR Swindon

Year Built
1961–1964

Engine
2 x Maybach MD655 rated at 1440 hp @ 1500 rpm built under licence by Bristol-Siddeley

Transmission
Hydraulic

BR Fleet Numbers
D1000–1073; TOPS = Class 52 (TOPS numbers never carried)

Notes: Although seven members of the class have been preserved, only D1015 *Western Champion* was preserved with the intent of returning it to the main line. This has been successfully achieved by the Diesel Traction Group (DTG), who are the owners of the locomotive, and the DTG limits the number of charters undertaken each year in order to protect its long-term future.

On 5 May 2003 D1015 *Western Champion* was hired by Pathfinder Tours to power the annual staff outing of Hanson, Mendip Rail and Foster Yeoman employees from Castle Cary to Llandudno Junction (for Llandudno) with the locomotive continuing to Penmaenmawr Quarry Sidings for servicing.

Above: D1015 *Western Champion* approaches Abergele on the outward journey.

Left: D1015 *Western Champion* stands in Penmaenmawr Quarry receiving attention whilst the coaching stock is serviced.

D1015 *Western Champion* skirts the North Wales Coast at Colwyn on the return journey.

D1015 *Western Champion* was hired to work a charter from Bristol–Carlisle on 3 September 2005 traversing both the WCML and S&C routes on the outward journey.

D1015 *Western Champion* curves through Leyland on its approach to Preston with the outward leg of a Bristol–Carlisle charter on 3 September 2005.

D1015 *Western Champion* passes Colton on 8 May 2008 running from its then base at Old Oak Common to Grosmont as guest visitor at a North Yorkshire Moors Railway (NYMR) Diesel Gala. En route D1015 called at Butterley to collect preserved Class 46 D182 and Barrow Hill to collect preserved Class 55 'Deltics' 55019 *Royal Highland Fusilier* and 55009 *Alycidon* for the NYMR event.

D1015 *Western Champion* nears the summit of Ais Gill on the outward journey of a Bristol-Carlisle charter on 3 September 2005.

D1015 *Western Champion* speeds through Edale on 20 March 2010 with a charter returning from Buxton to Bristol.

D1015 *Western Champion* made its first visit to Scotland on 3 May 2008 when it was hired to work a charter from Tame Bridge to Edinburgh travelling via the ECML on the outward journey and the WCML on the return journey.

D1015 *Western Champion* speeds past Spittal as it nears Edinburgh on the outward journey.

D1015 *Western Champion* speeds past Carrick Knowe Golf Course as it leaves Edinburgh under the shadow of Edinburgh Castle en route to Glasgow and its return to Tame Bridge via the WCML.

Class 55 – English Electric Company

Builder
English Electric (Vulcan Foundry)

Year Built
1961–1962

Engine
2 x Napier D18–25 rated at 1650 hp @ 1500 rpm

Transmission
Electric

BR Fleet Numbers
DELTIC; D9000–9021; TOPS = 55001–55022

The Deltic Preservation Society (DPS) bought three locomotives for preservation (D9009; D9015; 55019) with the hope of seeing at least one example work charters on the main line. The DPS succeeded in gaining accreditation for D9009 and 55019 which have subsequently seen occasional use on charter services.

D9009 *Alycidon* fires up ready to depart from Preston on 22 June 2003 with the DPS charter to Georgemas that was worked in top 'n tail mode with 55019 *Royal Highland Fusilier*.

D9009 *Alycidon* waits to leave Preston on 7 September 2002 with the empty stock of a terminating charter that was returning to its base at Carnforth (WCRC).

Preserved 55019 *Royal Highland Fusilier* **nears the summit of Copy Pit on 28 December 2005 whilst working an enthusiasts charter from York to Derby.**

D9016 *Gordon Highlander* **crosses Whalley Viaduct on 28 December 2003 with a Birmingham–Carlisle charter routed via the Ribble Valley and Settle & Carlisle routes.**

D9016 *Gordon Highlander* is a survivor from the ravages of Privatisation, having initially been sold to Deltic9000 Fund to provide spares for class doyen D9000 *Royal Scots Grey* which was being operated on the main line. In 2002 Porterbrook Leasing funded the overhaul of the locomotive subject to the proviso that the locomotive carry Porterbrook's purple livery.

Right: D9016 *Gordon Highlander* curves through Leyland on 30 December 2002 with a charter service from Derby to Carlisle.

Below: D9016 *Gordon Highlander* powers through Bamber Bridge on 28 September 2002 with a Newtown–Carlisle charter.

Class doyen D9000 *Royal Scots Grey* appeared to have a secure future when bought by Deltic9000 Fund and continued operating on the main line during the 1990s. Sadly the company entered administration in 2004 and the locomotive was offered for sale. Fortunately the locomotive was bought by Martin Walker, owner of Beaver Sports, and D9000 continues to see network operations – including occasional freight services.

Right: D9000 *Royal Scots Grey* powers away from Appleby on 18 May 2002 with a Cleethorpes–Carlisle charter.

Below Left: The NRM owns 55002 *Kings Own Yorkshire Light Infantry* but its return to working order was undertaken by NRM volunteers who gained main line certification for the locomotive during 2012. On 31 January 2014 the NRM sent 55002 to Carnforth (WCRC) to collect stock for transfer to its Shildon site; the return journey was noted curving away from Hellifield en route to Shildon.

Below Right: D9000/55022 *Royal Scots Grey* races through Brock on 4 March 2011 with a Carnforth (WCRC)–Preston stock move; at Preston the stock formed a Preston–Euston charter. The charter ran to provide a main line run for 'Deltic' Class 55 enthusiasts whilst utilising a stock move being operated to provide the trainset for a charter originating from London the following day.

In April 2011 GBRf hired D9000/55022 *Royal Scots Grey* for a short-term contract working a shuttle freight service from North Blyth to the Lynemouth Aluminium Smelter when it found itself with a temporary shortage of locomotives. The 'Deltic' was stabled at North Blyth during the period of the contract – and attracted much attention during its visit. On 19 April 2011 I made a visit to the area and took the following images.

Dawn breaks over Lynemouth as D9000/55022 *Royal Scots Grey* approaches Lynemouth smelter with the 06:00 North Blyth–Lynemouth service.

Once the tank wagons had been emptied they were returned to North Blyth as the 10:50 Lynemouth–North Blyth service. The train was required to stop at Freeman's Level Crossing where the double line was merged into a single line for the onward transit to North Blyth. These two images show D9000/55022 *Royal Scots Grey* approaching the stop signal at the level crossing.

Right: At North Blyth the 'Deltic' ran round the trainset to propel the wagons under the loading bay before detaching from the train whilst loading took place.

Below: Once the wagons were loaded the 'Deltic' shunted them into a train ready for a return to Lynemouth once a path could be given.

D9000/55022 *Royal Scots Grey* **passes Sleekburn Crossing with the empty wagons from Lynemouth to North Blyth.**

Such was the rarity of the operation that a further visit was made on 12 May 2011, resulting in the following images.

Above: D9000/55022 *Royal Scots Grey* crosses Wansbeck Bridge with the first North Blyth–Lynemouth service of the day.

Left: D9000/55022 *Royal Scots Grey* draws a loaded train out of the North Blyth loading facility onto the run-round loop prior to working to Lynemouth once a path for the train could be allocated.

Class 56 – Brush Traction; BR Workshops

Builder
Brush Traction; BR Crewe; BR Doncaster

Year Built
1976–1984

Engine
Ruston Paxman 16RK3CT rated at 3250 hp @ 900 rpm

Transmission
Electric

BR Fleet Numbers
56001–56135; 56301–56303; 56311–56312

Notes: The introduction of Class 66 locomotives by EWSR (English, Welsh and Scottish Railways) led to the early withdrawal of the Class 56 fleet but, once withdrawn, many locomotives had a second life as contractors' locomotives with High Speed Railway projects in France and Spain.

Within the UK some locomotives were bought for preservation whilst others were bought by Fastline and Colas Rail to begin operations as the first stage of their business plan. In the early days those locomotives returned to main line service were reclassified Class 56/3 but later purchases by Colas Rail (and others) retained their original BR numbers.

In 2005 Jarvis bought three Class 56 locomotives (56045/124/125 that were overhauled and renumbered 56301–3 respectively) to start Fastline Rail with an initial contract to move containers between Doncaster and the Isle of Grain and the hope of further contracts to transport coal to Ratcliffe Power Station for which it ordered five Class 66 locomotives.

When the company entered administration in 2010, 56301 was bought by the Class 56 Preservation Group which continued the main line operations by hiring it to railway operators/'spot hire' operators whilst the other duo were also bought for continued main line use.

Right: Fastline Class 56/3 56301 approaches the junction at Tupton on 5 July 2006 with the Doncaster–Isle of Grain container service.

When Fastline Rail entered administration, 56302 was bought by Class 56 enthusiast Ed Stevenson who then hired the locomotive to Colas Rail as part of its early hiring of locomotives as it sought to establish itself; Colas quickly had the locomotive re-liveried into the Colas Railfreight orange/black livery and branding.

Fastline Class 56/3 56302 curves through Portway on 20 January 2009 with the Doncaster–Thamesport container service.

Bearing Colas Railfreight livery, 56302 awaits departure from Ribblehead Sidings on 31 May 2013 with a timber service to Chirk.

The service from Ribblehead to Chirk must first head north to Blea Moor loop for the locomotive to run round the train then travel south via the Ribble Valley and the WCML to reach Chirk. On 31 May 2013 Class 56/3 56302 eases its train off the Ribblehead Viaduct after its reversal at Blea Moor en route to Chirk.

Class 56/3 56302 ambles through Euxton on 28 June 2013 with the Carlisle–Chirk timber service.

Class 56/3 56302 pilots Colas Class 56/0 56087 through Euxton on 10 June 2013 with the Carlisle–Chirk timber service.

Colas Class 56/0 56094 heads south through Brock on 2 February 2013 with the Carlisle–Chirk timber service.

In addition to the hire of Class 56/3 56302, Colas also bought Class 56/0 56032/049 /051/078/087/090/094/096/105/113 both as 'runners' and for spares. Those bought for operating services were painted in the orange/black house colours as they entered service after major overhaul to offset the lengthy periods of store that many locomotives had suffered.

Right: Diverted from the normal route due to engineering work between Crewe and Preston, Colas Class 56/0 56087 + 56105 pass through Buckshaw Parkway on 14 July 2013 with the return empty timber wagons from Chirk to Carlisle.

Below Right: In the early hours of 16 November 2012 Colas Class 56/0 56087 stands in Carlisle awaiting access to Kingmoor Siding with a special Teigngrace–Carlisle timber service.

Below Left: Colas Class 56/0 56113 races through Portway on 8 March 2016 with a Washwood Heath–Boston steel service.

The potential market for Class 56 locomotives led to some owners of preserved examples returning them to main line condition and hiring/selling them for network services. In 2008 Hanson Traction was established as a 'spot hire' locomotive operator which initially owned two Class 56 locomotives (56003/057 renumbered to 56312/11 respectively) that had been bought from their respective preservation owners. Hanson Traction was subsequently bought by BARS in 2010 and the latter company now operates the locomotives under the DCR banner.

Right: DCR Class 56/3 56312 *Artemis* pilots Class 66 66148 on 22 May 2010 as they approach Appleby with a Bristol–Carlisle charter.

Below: Hanson Traction Class 56/3 56312 *Artemis* works in top 'n tail mode with Class 67 67001 as they approach Ais Gill summit on 17 October 2009 with a Shrewsbury–Carlisle charter.

Ed Stevenson and Mark Winter joined forces to buy Class 56 locomotives which initially ran on heritage lines until the duo formed UKRL to offer 'spot hire' locomotives from a base at Leicester. On 8 March 2016 UKRL Class 56/0 56098 *The Lost Boys 1968–1988* was hired to move wagons from Cardiff Tidal to Derby Chaddesden Sidings, here seen passing Portway en route to Derby.

Class 57 – Brush Traction

Builder
Brush Traction

Year Built
1963–1967 (as Class 47)

Year Re-engineered
1997–2004

Engine
57/0 = General Motors 645-12E3 rated at 2500 hp @ 900 rpm; locomotives re-engineered
      1997–2000 for Freightliner
57/3 = General Motors 645-F3B rated at 2750 hp @ 900 rpm; locomotives re-engineered
      2002–2004 for Virgin Trains
57/6 = General Motors 645-12E3 rated at 2500 hp @ 900 rpm (57601); trial locomotive
      re-engineered 2001 for First Great Western
      General Motors 645-F3B rated at 2750 hp @ 900 rpm (57602–57605); production
      series re-engineered 2004 for First Great Western

Transmission
Electric

BR Fleet Numbers
57001–57012; 57301–57316; 57601–57605

Notes: The re-engineering programme was initiated by Porterbrook Leasings which sought to provide 'new' locomotives for Freightliner (Class 57/0) and Virgin Trains (Class 57/3) by re-engineering Class 47 locomotives rather than buying brand new ones. Although these 'new' locomotives are not 'heritage' by virtue of their rebuild date, they are 'heritage' by virtue of the use of Class 47 body shells hence their inclusion in this album. The selected photographs include examples of both the first lessee for whom the conversions were made and the subsequent operators who have either leased or bought the locomotives once the original leases to Freightliner and Virgin Trains were ended.

The conversion programme for the Class 57/0 fleet was undertaken in two batches with the original intention to reduce double-heading on the non-electrified branch line between Ipswich and Felixstowe, resulting in the need to change traction from electric to diesel on services to/from the port. This intent lasted only a short period before the fleet found wider use on Freightliner services as noted on 17 July 2002 when Class 57/0 57002 *Freightliner Phoenix* stood at Bootle Regent Rd waiting for permission to depart with its Seaforth FLT–Basford Hall 'trip' working.

Left: On 2 April 2003 Class 57/0 57001 *Freightliner Pioneer* curves through Seaforth Docks on its approach to Seaforth Terminal with a 'trip' working from Basford Hall.

Below Left: When its lease to Freightliner was ended, Class 57/0 57001 was bought by WCRC which used the locomotive on non-passenger duties as on 31 March 2011 when it was operated in top 'n tail mode with WCRC Class 47/8 47851 to collect Class 47/7 47768 from Barry for transfer to Carnforth (WCRC). The consist was noted passing Euxton with 57001 still waiting to receive WCRC's Maroon livery and branding.

Below Right: Class 57/0 57002 was re-leased to DRS which applied the 'Compass' house livery when it joined the DRS fleet. For a short period it was sub-leased to Colas Rail to power the Carlisle–Chirk timber service at the start of the latter's operations. When noted passing Winwick on 15 December 2009 with the Chirk–Carlisle service of empty wagons, the sub-lease was marked by the application of the Colas Insignia noted by the rear cab of 57002.

An early purchaser of Class 57/0 locomotives was Cotswold Rail which bought 57005/06 for its Advenza Freight operation but when the two companies entered administration the pair of locomotives were bought by WCRC for further use.

Class 57/0 57006 carries BR Corporate Blue livery and Advenza Freight branding on 2 July 2009 as it passes Portway with the Cardiff–Shipley service of empty wagons for scrap collection.

Class 57/0 57006 still bears its Advenza Freight branding on 18 July 2012, despite being owned by WCRC, as it provides rear-end insurance to A4 Class 4-6-2 60009 *Union of South Africa* during its main line test run round the Carnforth Circle (Carnforth–Hellifield–Blackburn–Preston–Carnforth).

Above Left: DRS Class 57/0 57008 *Telford International Railfreight Park June 2008* + 57004 amble past Brock on 1 July 2011 whilst working a Crewe–Sellafield flask service.

Above Right: DRS Class 57/0 57007 works in top 'n tail mode with DRS Class 47/7 47712 *Pride of Carlisle* as they leave Maryport on 25 May 2010 whilst working the 10:50 Maryport–Workington 'Floodex' service.

Left: DRS Class 57/0 57011 + 57007 power through Euxton on 28 June 2013 with a Coatbridge–Daventry service.

The Class 57/3 fleet was converted by Porterbrook Leasings to provide Virgin Trains with a locomotive capable of hauling the Pendelino and Voyager trainsets in times of failure and hauling Pendelino trainsets over non-electrified routes in cases of train diversions and service extensions (e.g. to Holyhead). Over time this need reduced and the locomotives were hired to other operators or, once the Virgin Trains leases were ended, sold or leased to other operators.

Class 57/3 locomotives leased to Virgin Trains were sub-hired to Arriva Trains Wales in 2006 to cover a Chester–Manchester–Holyhead–Manchester–Llandudno–Chester diagram during a shortage of Class 175 trainsets. On 21 July 2006 Class 57/3 57315 *The Mole* curved through Conway's battlements whilst working the Holyhead–Manchester Piccadilly link of the diagram.

Class 57/3 57306 *Jeff Tracey* assists failed Class 87/0 87013 *John of Gaunt* through Winwick on 18 June 2004 whilst working a Euston–Preston service.

Class 57/3 57309 *Brains* curves through Winwick on 2 April 2007 whilst on hire to Colas Rail to work the Carlisle–Chirk timber service whilst the latter company was sourcing its own fleet of locomotives to establish its train operating business.

Class 57/3 57305 *John Tracey* pilots failed Class 57/3 57314 *Firefly* out of Hellifield on 18 February 2006 whilst hauling Class 390 'Pendelino' trainset 390001 *Virgin Pioneer* that had been diverted over the Settle & Carlisle due to engineering works on the normal route between Carlisle and Preston.

WCRC Class 57/3 57313 curves through Beckfoot on 21 March 2015 whilst working a Didcot–Edinburgh charter in top 'n tail mode with Class 57/3 57315.

When Virgin Trains elected to relinquish its lease of Class 57/3 locomotives and the operation of the WCML 'Thunderbird' contract, some class members were sold to Network Rail and WCRC whilst others were re-leased to DRS. After a short period the Network Rail locomotives were transferred to DRS as the company identified other sources of traction for its needs. This resulted in DRS leasing 57301/03/05/06/10/12 and owning 57302/04/07/08/09/11 to service the Virgin Trains 'Thunderbird' contract and WCRC owning 57313–16.

WCRC Class 57/3 57316 bears the Arriva Trains Wales base blue livery, borne whilst on hire to the company, as it curves through Oubeck on 23 July 2014 whilst working a Hereford–Dundee charter in top 'n tail mode with Class 57/3 57314.

The NORTHERN BELLE haulage contract was gained by DRS during 2011 leading to Class 57/3 57305/312 receiving Pullman livery as part of the contract. On 23 March 2016 57312 *Solway Princess* was engaged in more mundane duty whilst piloting DRS Class 37/0 37069 through Winwick with a Crewe–Sellafield flask service.

Class 57/3 57308 *County of Staffordshire* takes a break from 'Thunderbird' duty on 6 July 2014 whilst working a Blackburn–Bradford Interchange shuttle service operated in conjunction with the Tour de France event taking place that weekend.

WCRC Class 57/6 57601 works in top 'n tail mode with WCRC Class 47/8 47854 *Diamond Jubilee* as they power through Bamber Bridge on 1 May 2013 with a Kidderminster–Carlisle charter.

Class 57/6 57601 was converted by Porterbrook as a trial for First Great Western but tests showed that a more powerful engine was needed, hence the 'production' batch of four locomotives adopted the same engine that was fitted to the Class 57/3 conversions. The trial locomotive was offered for sale and was bought by WCRC to supplement its fleet with its early workings being in connection with ROYAL SCOTSMAN duties.

Right: WCRC Class 57/6 57601 backs onto the 'Tin Bath' charter on 1 November 2015 at Manchester Victoria, after a pair of Class 5 4-6-0 steam locomotives had detached to return to their base on the ELR, prior to working the train forward to Preston thence empty stock to Carnforth (WCRC).

Below: WCRC Class 57/6 57601 passes Coed Kernow on 29 February 2004, bearing WCRC's early Maroon livery with Black Diamond Stripe, whilst approaching Cardiff with a Bolton–Cardiff charter run in conjunction with a Rugby match at Cardiff's Millennium Stadium.

Class 60 – Brush Traction

Builder
Brush Traction

Year Built
1989–1993

Engine
Mirrlees 8MB275T rated at 3100 hp @ 1000 rpm

Transmission
Electric

BR Fleet Numbers
60001–60100

Notes: The class was severely affected by the arrival of Class 66 locomotives with many class members being stored as they became due for overhaul, although eleven class members were given major overhauls by EWS/DB Schenker to work some of its heaviest freight services. After lengthy periods in store DB Schenker offered ten locomotives for sale in 2014 (60002/21/26/47/56/76/85/87/95/96) and these were bought by Colas Rail as it sought to build up its locomotive fleet.

Colas Class 60 60087 *CLIC Sargent* pilots Colas Class 66/8 66849 *Wylam Dilly* through Whalley on 28 May 2015 whilst working a Carlisle–Chirk timber service.

Right: Colas Class 60 60002 curves through Lostock Hall Junction on 25 March 2015 whilst working a Preston Dock–Lindsey Oil Refinery service of empty bitumen tank wagons.

Below Left: Colas Class 60 60026 curves onto the main line at Balshaw Lane Junction on 27 May 2016 whilst working a Carlisle–Chirk timber service.

Below Right: Colas Class 60 60085 crawls towards an adverse signal at Preston in the early hours of 28 August 2015 whilst working a Chirk–Carlisle service of empty timber wagons.

Class 73 – BR Eastleigh C&W; English Electric Company

Builder
BR Eastleigh C&W; English Electric (Vulcan Foundry)

Year Built
1962–1966

Power Source
Diesel English Electric 4SRKT rated at 600 hp @ 850 rpm
Electric 3rd Rail 750 V DC/1600 hp

Transmission
Electric

BR Fleet Numbers
E6001–6049; TOPS = See note below

Notes: The first six locomotives were built to a BR Southern Region specification by Eastleigh C&W because many of the component parts were available as part of EMU construction. Such was their value that the Bournemouth Electrification Scheme (1967) included the construction of a further forty-three examples, with detail differences, that were built by English Electric. In 1984 a batch of twelve locomotives was dedicated to the 'Gatwick Express' service between London Victoria and Gatwick Airport but problems were quickly caused by frequent high-speed running; this was solved by re-gearing the locomotives which subsequently became classified as Class 73/2.

When EWS bought the freight companies after Privatisation, an early decision was to withdraw the Class 73 fleet but some were bought for preservation whilst many were bought by other companies for continued network use.

TOPS Classification: The introduction of TOPS in the late 1960s and its application to Fleet Operations from 1974 allowed various sub-groups to be identified; these were enhanced by further sub-groups after Privatisation hence the current TOPS classifications include:

73.0 = Original six locomotives
73.1 = English Electric build with detail differences
73.2 = Gatwick Express locomotives with altered gearing
73.9 = 73951–952; locomotives re-engineered 2013–2016 for Network Rail by RVEL at Derby replacing 4SRKT engine by 2 x Cummins QSK19 rated at 750 hp @ 1800 rpm
73.9 = 73961–971; locomotives re-engineered 2014–2016 for GB Railfreight by Brush Traction replacing 4SRKT engine by MTU 8V4000 R43L rated at 1600 hp @1800 rpm

73951–952 have yet to enter service as at December 2016 hence no sphere of operations has been identified
73961–965 are dedicated to Network Rail services in the South East of England
73966–971 are dedicated to Serco Caledonian Sleeper services from Edinburgh to Aberdeen/Fort William/Inverness.

North of London the Merseyrail Network provides a rare sighting of Class 73 traction where the 3rd rail and non-electrified lines prove little problem for overnight inspection of the system.

Network Rail Class 73/1 73138 arrives at Southport in the early hours of 29 March 2014 working in top 'n tail mode with GBRf Class 73/2 73201 *Broadlands* on a Merseyrail Inspection Train.

A year earlier on 9 March 2013, 73138 was in top 'n tail mode with GBRf Class 73/1 73107 *Redhill 1844–1994* as they waited to continue to Ormskirk via Sandhills.

GBRf Class 73/2 locomotives stabled in Eastleigh station yard on 13 March 2011 included 73213 and 73212 (still bearing modified First Group livery) and 73208 *Kristen* in BR's Corporate Blue livery.

GBRf Class 73/2 73201 *Broadlands* awaits departure from Southport on 29 March 2014 with a Network Rail Inspection train to Ormskirk via Sandhills, working in top 'n tail mode with Network Rail Class 73/1 73138.

On 29 July 2015 GBRf Class 73/9 73961 *Alison* + 73963 *Janice* made a rare visit north to Crewe where they ran in top 'n tail mode between Crewe and Warrington to test their Electric Train Heat equipment; on the outward journey 73961 *Alison* was leading as the test consist passed Acton Bridge.

Top Right: Another rare sighting occurred in March 2016 when GBRf Class 73/9 73969 + 73968 were sent to Carnforth (WCRC) to collect the ROYAL SCOTSMAN trainset for transfer to Bo'ness, the normal base for the stock during the operating season. On 18 March 2016 the duo joined the main line at the start of their northbound journey, travelling via Kilmarnock to collect further stock from the trainset.

Bottom Left: The GBRf Class 73/9s began working Caledonian Sleeper services in June 2016 and in the early hours of 22 July 2016 73966 + 73968 waited to depart from Edinburgh Waverley with the Fort William portion of the HIGHLANDER Caledonian Sleeper service. Of interest is that 73966/73967 were re-engineered from Class 73/0 E6005/73005 and E6006/73006 respectively; they had been sold into preservation and had been bought back from the owner by GBRf specifically for the re-engineering programme.

Bottom Right: Problems with the GBRf Class 73/9 alternators led to Caledonian Sleeper services being powered by a combination of GBRf Class 66/7 and Class 73/9 with the Class 73/9 attached to the coaching stock for train heating purposes. In the early hours of 22 July 2016 the Inverness portion of the HIGHLANDER Caledonian Sleeper service waited to depart behind Class 66/7 66737 *Leisa* leading Class 73/9 73969.

Class 86 – BR Doncaster; English Electric Company

Builder
BR Doncaster; English Electric (Vulcan Foundry)

Year Built
1965–1966

Power Source/Rating
25 kV AC Overhead/5000 hp (Class 86/1); 4000 hp (All other sub-groups)

Transmission
Electric

BR Fleet Numbers
E3101–3200; TOPS = See note below

Notes: The Class 86 design emanated from the experience of the five 1st Generation designs (TOPS = 81–85) supplied by various manufacturers to a BR specification and, from which experience, a new specification was drafted. In practice the choice of axle-hung traction motors rather than the nose-suspended option used with the earlier Classes 81–85 led to problems and the creation over time of sub-classes. The AC Locomotive Group (ACLG) had set the objective of preserving an example of each AC locomotive class when withdrawn from service and succeeded in preserving an example of one of each from Classes 81–85 and have continued with the preservation of Classes 86/1; 86/2; 86/4; 87/0 and 89.

The ACLG's aim is to have working examples and in 2007 it succeeded in gaining main line certification for its Class 86/1 86101 *Sir William Stanier FRS* and Class 87/0 87002 *Royal Sovereign*. These were hired by GBRf for (staff) charter work then, as part of its contract to supply electric traction for the Caledonian Sleeper service, GBRf hired 86101 *Sir William Stanier FRS*, 86401 and 87002 *Royal Sovereign* for empty stock moves with the contingency that both 86101 and 87002 could power the sleeper trains in emergency.

The income from the GBRf contract is being used by the ACLG to fund the restoration of Class 89 89001 and as this album is compiled work still continues on its restoration with the hope that mainline certification (and service) will follow.

TOPS Classification: The introduction of TOPS in the late 1960s and its application to Fleet Operations from 1974 allowed various sub-groups to be identified; these were enhanced by further sub-groups after Privatisation hence the current TOPS classifications include:

86.0 = 86001–86038 locomotives fitted with freight gearing and restricted operating speed

86.1 = 86101–86103 locomotives fitted with class 87 bogies

86.2 = 86203–86262 locomotives fitted with modified suspension for passenger work

86.3 = 86301–86338 (re-engineered 86001–86038 with gaps) locomotives fitted with modified wheel sets for freight duty

86.4 = 86401–86438 (re-engineered 86001–86038 (remaining) + 86301–86338) locomotives fitted with improved suspension

86.5 = 86501–86508 locomotives temporarily restricted to freight duties with Railfreight Distribution before restoration to Class 86/2 specification and numbering
86501 re-engineered Class 86/6 86608 modified to Class 90 specification by Freightliner but restored to Class 86/6 specification and number in 2016

86.6 = A number of class 86/4 with modified suspension and speed restricted to 75 mph for freight duty

86.7 = 2 Class 86/2 locomotives modified for 110 mph operation by Europhoenix and offered as 'spot hire' traction

86.9 = 2 Class 86/2 locomotives bought by Network Rail for load bank testing then subsequently used for OHLE clearance of ice/snow during winter

Right: Class 86/1 86101 *Sir William Stanier FRS* made its return to main line service on 24 March 2007 when it worked the Carlisle–Crewe leg of a Carlisle–Holyhead charter in top 'n tail mode with Riviera Trains Class 47/8 47815 *Great Western*; 86101 was 'panned' as it passed Euxton Junction on the outward journey.

Below Left: Class 86/1 86101 *Sir William Stanier FRS* was often hired by GBRf to assist its mail train workings as on 4 December 2008 when it was used to haul a trio of Class 325 Royal Mail trainsets with traction motor problems; the consist was noted curving through Leyland whilst hauling a Willesden PRMT–Shieldmuir service.

Below Right: Although normally used for Caledonian Sleeper stock movements between Euston and Wembley, Class 86/1 86101 *Sir William Stanier FRS* can be used on the normal service in emergency as in the early hours of 28 August 2015 when it waited for the signal to depart from Preston with the southbound LOWLANDER service to Euston.

Class 86/1 86101 *Sir William Stanier FRS* + Class 87/0 87002 *Royal Sovereign* curve through Winwick on 21 November 2008 with a stock move from Carnforth (WCRC) to Doncaster as a prelude to working a GBRf staff charter the following day.

Shortly before being withdrawn from service, Class 86/2 86259 was named *Les Ross* in dedication to a Birmingham-based radio presenter who was retiring after many years' service. After his retirement he bought the locomotive when it was offered for sale; it was based at Willesden depot for a time to power charters originating from Euston but at the end of December 2016 it was moved to Tyseley depot from its previous base at Willesden.

Right: An early outing for 86259 *Les Ross* was on 1 March 2008 from Tyseley, where it was initially based, working a Tyseley–Preston charter in top 'n tail mode with Vintage Trains Class 47/7 47773. Part of the charter involved a Preston–Crewe stock movement for servicing, here seen passing Balshaw Lane Junction on the outward journey.

Below Left: On 25 August 2011 86259 *Les Ross* was used on a similar working and was noted passing Euxton on the southbound journey working the return Carnforth–Euston leg.

Below Right: Once moved to Willesden, it was dedicated to steam workings in the north of England, working the Euston–Carnforth leg, as on 14 June 2012 when 86259 *Les Ross* curved through Oubeck on its approach to Lancaster en route to Carnforth where the steam traction took over for the journey to Carlisle.

Right: The ACLG, through Electric Traction Services (ETS), its commercial company, modified a pair of Class 86/2s for 110 mph operation (86205/60 that became 86701/02 respectively) which were re-liveried, reclassified Class 86/7 and offered for 'spot hire'. The hire was taken up by GB Railfreight to haul the Royal Mail's Class 325 trainsets when the latter suffered traction problems, as on 8 January 2010 when Class 86/7 86702 *Cassiopeia* was noted passing Euxton hauling a Shieldmuir–Willesden PRMT mail service.

Below Left: Class 86/2 86259 *Les Ross* made history on 20 December 2008 when it became the first 25kV AC locomotive to work a train over the Woodhead Route following its conversion from the original 15kV DC overhead system. Working the outward leg of the Manchester Piccadilly–Hadfield service, supplementing the main Birmingham New St–Manchester Piccadilly charter, 86259 curves off Dinting Viaduct on the direct route (omitting Glossop) as it approaches Hadfield.

Below Right: In 2013 Colas Railfreight hired Class 86/7 86701 to trial a freight service between Daventry and London Euston that came to naught but which saw 86701 re-liveried into Colas colours. At the end of the trial the pair of Class 86/7s were moved to Barrow Hill for storage pending negotiations that saw them sold to a Bulgarian train operator during 2014. During a visit to Barrow Hill on 6 February 2014 the duo were noted stabled atop the ACLG's preserved Class 82 and 89 locos in a line-up that comprised (from left to right) Class 89 89001; Class 82 82008; Class 86/7 86702 *Cassiopeia* and Class 86/7 86701 *Orion*.

Shortly after the passage of the southbound Shieldmuir–Willesden PRMT mail service on 8 January 2010 (see opposite page), the corresponding northbound Willesden PRMT–Shieldmuir service passed Euxton behind Class 86/7 86701 *Orion* hauling three Class 325 Royal Mail trainsets.

Class 87 – BREL Crewe

Builder
BR Crewe

Year Built
1973–1975

Power Source/Rating
25 kV AC Overhead/5000 hp

Transmission
Electric

BR Fleet Numbers
87001–87035; 87101

Notes: The Class 87 fleet was built as the premier traction for the Weaver Junction–Glasgow Central electrification scheme and continued at work until withdrawal by Virgin Trains when replacement Class 390 'Pendelino' trainsets were introduced from 2003. The final official working was in June 2005 when a Euston–Birmingham–Manchester Piccadilly 'Farewell to Class 87' charter was operated. The traction on the day included 87002 *AC Locomotive Group* to commemorate the fact that the ACLG had been promised the locomotive by Porterbrook once withdrawn. This added the locomotive to the ACLG's collection of AC locomotives which are preserved at Barrow Hill.

The ACLG's aim is to have working examples and in 2007 it succeeded in gaining main line certification for 87002 *Royal Sovereign* and Class 86/1 86101 *Sir William Stanier FRS*. These were hired by GBRf for (staff) charter work but as part of its contract to supply electric traction for the Caledonian Sleeper service, GBRf hired 86101, 86401 and 87002 for empty stock moves with the contingency that both 86101 and 87002 could power the sleeper trains in emergency.

The income from the GBRf contract is being used by the ACLG to fund the restoration of Class 89 89001 and as this album is being compiled work still continues on its restoration with the hope that mainline certification (and service) will follow.

TOPS Classification: The introduction of TOPS in the late 1960s and its application to Fleet Operations from 1974 allowed various sub-groups to be identified:

87/0 = 87001–87035 production series
87/1 = 87101 test locomotive fitted with thyristor equipment

Once released by Virgin Trains back to Porterbrook, the Class 87 fleet suffered mixed fortunes as Porterbrook sought to find work for them before most class members were sold to Bulgarian operators for further service abroad. In the interim GBRf arranged a short-term contract to operate Class 87/0 locomotives as 'Thunderbirds' with the Class 325 Royal Mail trainsets that were part of the Royal Mail contract gained by GBRf in 2004. The locomotives operated under this contract retained the liveries they carried when released by Virgin Trains and observations included:

87019 *ACORP Association of Community Rail Partnerships* hauling a consist of four Class 325 trainsets through Lowton on 24 April 2006 with a Shieldmuir–Warrington RMT service.

87006 hauls three Class 325 Royal Mail trainsets through Leyland on 10 April 2006 whilst working a Shieldmuir–Warrington RMT service.

87012 *Olympian* hauls Class 325 trainset 325012 through Leyland on 11 July 2005 whilst working a Shieldmuir–Warrington RMT service.

87002 *AC Locomotive Group* bears Porterbrook livery on 13 April 2006 whilst hauling three Class 325 Royal Mail trainsets past Euxton on a Shieldmuir–Warrington RMT service.

87022 hauls three Class 325 Royal Mail trainsets through Euxton on 21 April 2006 whilst working a Shieldmuir–Warrington RMT service.

Restored to BR Corporate blue livery, Class 87/0 87002 *Royal Sovereign* was one of three locomotives hired from the ACLG by GBRf to power stock movements in conjunction with the Caledonian Sleeper service. On occasions 87002 is called upon to work the main service as in the early hours of 30 April 2015 when 87002 entered Preston with the southbound HIGHLANDER Caledonian Sleeper service (comprising Aberdeen/Fort William and Inverness portions) en route to Euston.

Class 89 – Brush Traction/BR Workshops

Builder
BREL Crewe

Year Built
1986

Power Source/Rating
25 kV AC Overhead/5850 hp

Transmission
Electric

BR Fleet Numbers
89001

Note: This locomotive was designed by Brush Traction but built by BREL Crewe then trialled on both the WCML and ECML routes with the hope that orders would be placed for a production series as part of the East Coast Main Line (ECML) electrification. In the event, BR elected to adopt the Class 91 + MkIV combination that, as at 2016, still provides the staple traction of the route, although 89001 provided early motive power for the route, albeit confined to Kings Cross–Leeds services until the arrival of the Class 91 fleet. In 1992 it suffered major failure and, as BR considered its purchase to have been part of the cost of electrifying the ECML, it was withdrawn from service then entered preservation by Brush Traction engineers at the Midland Railway Centre.

The locomotive returned to mainline service in 1997 when the ECML was privatised and Great North Eastern Railway (GNER), the operating company, faced a motive power shortage in 1996 hence found it economic to repair the locomotive and return it to service on a Kings Cross–Leeds diagram. This operated until 2001 when the locomotive suffered further failure and, being a one-off, the cost of repairs led to the decision to withdraw the locomotive from service once more. After a lengthy period in store 89001 was passed to the ACLG at Barrow Hill in December 2004 for secure storage but was subsequently bought by the group when the locomotive was put up for sale by tender in 2006.

The ACLG has since sought to restore the locomotive and, as at December 2016, this is being achieved by using the income from the contract with GBRf for locomotives to service the stock movements of the Caledonian Sleeper service. During 2016 the major components have been inspected and renewed/repaired as appropriate whilst the ACLG continues the overhaul programme with aspiration of a return to main line service in due course.

89001 bears its original BR Inter City livery on 23 September 2015 as it stables at Barrow Hill awaiting the start of the overhaul that will, hopefully, see its return to the national network on passenger duty.

Class 92 – Brush Traction

Builder
Brush Traction

Year Built
1993–1996

Power Source/Rating
25 kV AC Overhead/6760 hp; 750 v DC 3rd Rail/5360 hp

Transmission
Electric

BR Fleet Numbers
92001–92046

Notes: The Class 92 fleet was originally supplied to three companies involved with the construction and operation of the Channel Tunnel–BR Railfreight Distribution (30 locomotives), French National Railways (9 locomotives) and European Passenger Services (7 locomotives). Their introduction proved troublesome as French unions objected to them on grounds of safety and complexity; the planned passenger services were cancelled and their operation within the UK affected signalling circuits leading to class members being banned from certain routes.

The class has been included in this album because of the age of class members (+20 years) and because class members have passed through various ownerships until reaching the status as at August 2016 whereby DB Schenker (DBS) owns 30 locomotives and Europorte owns 16 locomotives. DBS operates 6 of its fleet on Channel Tunnel traffics hence are rarely seen north of London and the remainder are split with 12 locomotives now operated by DBS companies in Bulgaria and Romania and 12 locomotives stored at Crewe Electric Depot. Europorte was formed by Eurotunnel in 2007 to operate freight services and bought GB Railfreight (GBRf) in 2010 to operate services within the UK, including the operation of the Class 92s. Europorte subsequently sold GBRf to the Swedish-owned Hector Rail in November 2016 when the status of the fleet was that 10 locomotives were operational whilst 6 were retained as a source of spares.

92043 *DeBussey* **approaches Manchester Oxford Road on 3 July 2013, bearing its Europorte branding, whilst working a Trafford Park–Felixstowe service.**

GBRf operates the daily Halewood–Dagenham–Halewood service which, on 27 August 2014, was powered by 92010 *Molière* noted passing Acton Bridge on the southbound journey.

In 2014 GBRf was contracted to provide motive power for Serco's Caledonian Sleeper service which began on April 1 2015. The second of the two northbound services each night is the LOWLANDER service (Euston–Glasgow Central/Edinburgh) which was powered by 92033 when noted at Preston in the early hours of 30 April 2015 bearing the livery adopted by Serco for its Caledonian Sleeper service.

Soon after the Class 92 locomotives began powering the Caledonian Sleeper service, the locomotives quickly fell foul of the WCML OHLE when the latter's tolerances for power supplies proved greater than that of the locomotives. This required replacement by contracted Freightliner Class 90s whilst the problems were resolved. 92014 was returned to Brush Traction at Loughborough where modifications were applied then released to traffic in June 2016 for testing.

The test programme proved the success of the modifications; from August 2016 these were applied to other class members which were then scheduled to resume duties on the sleeper services from January 2017 and release the contracted Class 90s back to Freightliner.

Opposite: The first trials were held between Crewe and Liverpool with 92014 piloting the train locomotive of the Garston–Dagenham service as far as Crewe where the train locomotive continued; on 8 June 2016 92014 passed Runcorn with GBRf Class 66/7 66720 as the train locomotive.

Right: The final stage was the return of 92014 to service on the Caledonian Sleeper service, albeit restricted to the LOWLANDER (Euston–Glasgow Central/Edinburgh) service as noted in the early hours of 9 July 2016 when 92014 waited to depart from Preston with the southbound working.

Below: When the 1st stage trials were thought complete the next stage was a series of runs with stock that operated in top 'n tail mode with 92010 on 15 June 2016. 92014 powered the test train, which was 'panned' passing Winwick on the Carnforth–Rugby leg of the trial runs.

GBRf operates a Network Rail service between Mossend and Carlisle which is normally hauled by a Class 92 locomotive – as on 13 May 2016 when 92032 *IMechE Railway Division*, the only class member to carry GBRf livery with Europorte branding, passed Dinwoodie whilst working the return Carlisle–Mossend service.